What It Means to be Born Again

Rodney M. Howard-Browne

AF539697

RHBEA Publications
P.O. Box 197161, Louisville, KY 40259-7161 U.S.A.
P.O. Box 3900, Randburg 2125 South Africa

Unless otherwise indicated, all scriptural references are from the *King James Version* of the Bible.

Second Printing, July 1993

What It Means to be Born Again
ISBN 0-9583066-1-3
Copyright © 1992 by Rodney M. Howard-Browne

Published by RHBEA Publications
P.O. Box 197161, Louisville, KY 40259-7161 U.S.A.
P.O. Box 3900, Randburg 2125 South Africa

Cover design and book production by
DB & Associates Design Group, Inc.
P.O. Box 52756
Tulsa, OK 74152

Printed in the United States of America

All rights reserved under International Copyright Law. Contents and/or cover may not be reproduced in whole or in part in any form without the express written consent of the publisher.

What It Means to be Born Again

Chapter 1

Understanding the New Birth Experience

For God so loved the world, that he gave his only begotten Son, that whosoever believeth in him should not perish, but have everlasting life.

John 3:16

Building Your Life on a Firm Foundation

I believe that there needs to be a greater understanding of the basic truths of the Bible in the Church today. When foundational truths are burned in our spirit, there's no devil in hell, no false doctrine, no deceiver that can come and sway us away from the purpose and the plan and the will of God for our lives.

One of the reasons why people backslide and grow cold in their Christian experience is because the basic truths have never been branded inside them. Everywhere we go, we find people coming to recommit their lives to God.

Belonging to a church does not make you a child of God just as working in an automobile factory does not make you an automobile. I don't care who the person is. I don't care how long they've been in the church. I don't care if they were the founding members of that church. Just because they belong to a church does not make them a Christian.

In the United States, people are under a misconception. They think that America is a Christian nation. And they think because they're not a Jew or a Muslim, they're a Christian.

I've got news for them. Unless you are born again of the Spirit of God, you're not a Christian. And the problem about that is you're going to split hell wide open. That's a bold statement, but it must be said. We must challenge others concerning the new birth.

The Lord said to me once, *Don't take for granted that a person is born again even if they wear a big badge saying, "Smile, if you love Jesus," and have a big bumper sticker on their car and carry a Bible big enough to choke a donkey and they walk around quoting scripture. Don't ever take for granted that they're born again.*

I asked the Lord, "Why are there hundreds of people coming to the altar at our services? The churches are filled with thousands of people, but some are the biggest kooks in the business." The Lord said to me, *Many of them are not even born again. They've never had a new birth experience. They've never come to the foot of the cross. They've stood in the line and said, "Jesus, I confess You as my*

Lord and Savior." But, they've never had a change of heart.

The new birth is not external. Salvation is not mental. Salvation is of the heart, and when man comes with the heart and accepts Jesus Christ as his Lord and Savior, he's born again. He's changed. He becomes a new creature in Christ Jesus. That's the exciting thing about the new birth.

Second Corinthians 5:17 says, "Therefore if any man be in Christ, he is a new creature: old things are passed away; behold, all things become new." Not he thinks he is, not maybe he is, but he *is* a new creature. That literally means a new species of being that has never existed before. When you're born again, old things are passed away.

Don't tell me you're born again and you still live like you did before you were born again. I will not believe you. I don't care if you go to the First Church of Whatever. I don't care if your father's the deacon. I don't care if you're the head elder. I don't care if you're on so many boards that you're bored. When you are born again, you are changed. You become new.

People who think they can be born again and live just the way they always did are fooling themselves. Their hearts are not right with God, but they have camouflaged it so well they don't realize it. They have never come to the place of repentance.

In fact, there are some people today who think God got Himself a deal because He got them. They think God owed them salvation.

God didn't owe us anything. The whole crux of Christianity is God reached down to a lost and dying world. He came down to restore man back to what Adam lost in the Garden of Eden. God came through Jesus Christ to restore mankind back to their rightful place. But God didn't have to do it.

He could have let us all go to hell. But because of His love extended toward us while we were yet sinners, the Bible says Christ died for us (Romans 5:8). He knew who we were.

Many are coming to church and merely praying a mental prayer. But saying the right words does not cause the new birth to take place. Something must happen inside. There must be a time where you know you crossed the line.

The Bible says we know we have crossed from death unto life because we love the brethren (First John 3:14). We know. Not we think so, not we hope so, not maybe so. We know that we passed from death unto life because we love the brethren. There's a dividing line we cross over.

You were once lost and now you are found. You were once blind and now you see. You were once in darkness and now you're in the light. He took us and translated us out of the kingdom of darkness and brought us into the kingdom of His dear Son (Colossians 1:13). You were once in the family of the wicked one; now you're in the family of God. There's a whole transition. It's like leaving one country and going to another.

It's important to recognize this because thousands merely mentally assent and say, "Yes, I accept Jesus Christ as my Lord and Savior." But they go out the door and continue to live the life of a sinner. It grieves the Spirit of God.

This is the reason why so many backslide today. They have never had a true new birth experience. We've made it so easy to become born again. Come and join the club.

Today being born again is a fashionable thing. Are you born again? "I'm born again but I tell you what, I'm going to sue that guy for everything he's got. I'm born again, but I'm going to kill that guy." The Bible says if you can't even love your brother whom you can see, how can you love God who you cannot see (First John 4:20)?

Today in many churches with five to ten thousand members, there could be as many as 40 percent who are not born again. They may have come for five or ten years to those churches, but there has been no change in their lives. They continue the same old life. They continue to speak the same language. They work the same crooked deals. They commit the same sins.

I'm not talking about people who have a moment of weakness or get tripped up by the devil. I'm talking about people who habitually sin. The Bible says whoever is born of God doesn't sin, meaning that they don't practice it as a way of life (First John 3:9). When you practice sin as a way of life, how can you be born again?

If you sin and you know you've done wrong, immediately you can feel it in your heart. I look at some people and say, "If they're born again, how do they sleep at night?" I couldn't sleep at night if I were doing the things they are doing.

It's frightening to think that there could be as many as 40 percent, and in some churches as high as 80 percent, who are not born again. They dress up in a suit on Sunday, carry a Bible big enough to choke a donkey, go to church, sing hymns and put in an offering, yet they're not born again. Jesus said, "Ye must be born again" (John 3:7).

And the worst thing is to think that because you grew up in a Christian family and your father was a preacher and you've gone to church all your life, you're automatically born again. There are some young people who grew up in the church but they've never had a new birth experience.

I was born again at the age of 5. I went to the altar and made a commitment, but I had several experiences between the time I was 5 and the time I was 18 years old. At that time, I had an encounter with God so that I knew without a shadow of a doubt I was born again.

I remember one night having a dream. I don't talk about this much, but it is (refreshed) in my memory every now and then. I was about 13 years of age and I remember I had a dream in which I saw Jesus.

We used to have little tracts with a picture of millions of people going over a cliff and falling into the flames of hell. There was a road going up on the side and the cross. This left an impression on me. I'd always picture myself going up that road.

The Bible says, "Broad is the way, that leadeth to destruction, and many there be which go in thereat: Because strait is the gate, and narrow is the way, which leadeth unto life" (Matthew 7:13, 14). There are 260 million people in the United States and they estimate — these are figures put out by religious organizations — that 60 million are born again. That means 200 million people in the United States do not know Jesus Christ as Lord and Savior. This country — the United States of America — is one of the greatest overlooked mission fields on the face of God's green earth.

I remember as a child looking at that tract. In my dream, I was standing right there and I saw the millions of people going over into the flames. I remember crying — I don't know how long it was. It seemed like two and a half hours. But I woke up and my pillow was soaking wet.

Jesus was standing right there. I can't remember what He looked like, but I knew it was Jesus because I was talking to Him. I said, "O Jesus, what can we do? There are millions of people going to a lost eternity." I heard Him say, "You must tell them. You must tell them. You must tell them."

I woke up and the next day when I went outside, everything was new. It was an experience I'll never forget. I began to witness then even more to the kids at school. I began to tell them about the Lord Jesus and about His coming.

It was from this experience that I knew it wasn't just something that my father had, or my mother had, or my uncle had. I knew it was something I had. The new birth was real to me. Jesus was real to me and I wanted Him to become real to other people. When God gives you that, something will arise on the inside of you that will cause you to share the Gospel of the Lord Jesus Christ.

There's something that will cause you to leave everything you have — to forsake houses and lands, to leave a job, and turn your back on everything else when you know about the truth of the gospel of the Lord Jesus Christ. That something, that truth burned deep into your heart, will cause you to go through blizzards, earthquakes, famines, and wars to obey the call of God. You'll not quit until you see what God has called you to do.

If things don't go right in the ministry of some people, they quit. They say, "I'm quitting. I'm leaving the ministry."

I'm so glad when Jesus hung on the cross He didn't say, "I'm quitting." I'm so glad in the Garden of Gethsemane He didn't say, "That's it, Father. Enough is enough." The Bible says He could have called 10,000 angels to rescue Him away, but I'm so glad He didn't. He looked down through the eons of time and He saw you and me. He said, "I will pay the price. I will buy them back. I will shed My blood for their redemption."

Second Corinthians 5:21 says, "He hath made him to be sin for us, who knew no sin; that we might be made the righteousness of God in him." Jesus became sin for you and me because we were sinners. He became sin that you and I could be born again into the family of God.

Someone asked me, "Brother Rodney, what must I do to come to God? Must I change my life first and then come to Him?" No! You come as you are. God wants you as you are. God specializes in taking us "as is."

Have you ever seen cars advertised "as is"? God said, "Give me that sinner there, 'as is,' and watch what I will do." He'll take a prostitute, a drug addict, a homosexual, a down-and-out criminal who is full of sin and He will transform that person in a moment, in the twinkling of an eye. He will change them and He will put their feet on higher ground. He will wash them in the blood of Jesus. He will cleanse them and they'll be like a brand new little baby that has just been born.

That's what the new birth is. God wants to restore back to the Church the joy of their salvation. Some Christians have forgotten why they were saved. They've forgotten that they were saved. If you looked at some Christians, you couldn't even tell they were born again. "Well I'm saved, Brother Rodney." Saved from what? God wants to restore you. I pray that you get a fresh revelation of the new birth.

Chapter 2

My Name Is Written Down

The disciples came to Jesus after He had sent them out to minister. They were so excited, they were jumping up and down. "O, Jesus, isn't it wonderful? Demons are subject to us through Your name. We've been casting out devils and you know what, they listen to us."

Jesus said, in effect, "So what. I beheld Satan as lightening fall from heaven. He's defeated. Don't rejoice over the fact that demons are subject to you, but rejoice over the fact that your name is written down in the Lamb's Book of Life." (See Luke 10:17-20.)

My name is written down in the Lamb's Book of Life! My name may not be down in Who's Who in the Zoo. My name may not be down on this roll and that roll and the bank roll. But my name is written down "when the roll is called up yonder." And I'm going to be there!

I'm part of the family of God. I've been bought with a price. I've been brought out of darkness into light. I'm an ambassador from the kingdom of heaven. I have my passport made out. My visa's stamped in the blood of Jesus. I have first-class air tickets. I'm sitting on Rapture Airlines. The flight attendant is serving me living water, and the new wine, and heaven's bread. That's something to get excited about.

We don't serve a dead God. We don't serve a God who's deaf. We don't serve a God who's blind. We don't serve a God who has no power. Our God is still God. He's the same God of Moses and Elijah and Daniel. And He's alive in 1992. He wants to manifest Himself in 1992.

Too much importance has been placed on what church you belong to. "Well, I'm of Paul and I'm of Apollos," we say. "We have a 5,000-seat church and a thousand-voice choir. And you should see our deacons. They can deke like no other dekes. Our elders can eld like no other. Our church board is one of the boardest boards in the city. We've got an orchestra. And have you heard our pipe organ?" Well, who cares?

It doesn't matter what church you belong to. It matters what family you belong to. You are in either one of two families. You're either in the family of the devil or you're in the family of God.

To be born again is not confirmation. "I've been through confirmation, Brother Rodney." Well, wonderful. Have you been born again? Jesus never said, "Ye must be confirmed." Jesus said, "Ye must be born again."

"Well, Brother Rodney, I've been to catechism." You can't "ism" it any other way. Have you been born again?

"Well, Brother Rodney, we joined the church. We filled in a membership." Jesus never said, "Ye must fill in a church membership. Ye must put thy name on the roll." He said, "Ye must be born again."

"Well, Brother Rodney, we've been baptized in water." You can live under water till you get webbed feet. But I'm telling you right now Jesus didn't say, "Go under water." He said, "Ye must be born again."

"Well, Brother Rodney, we had some water sprinkled on our head." You can have water sprinkled on your head until you grow a plant. He didn't say, "Ye must get water sprinkled on your head." He said, "Ye must be born again."

"Well, Brother Rodney, we take communion. Every week we have the Holy Sacrament." You can swallow grape juice or wine and wafers three times a day. He didn't say, "Ye must take communion." He said, "Ye must be born again."

"Well, Brother Rodney, we observe religious duties. We go to church regularly every Sunday morning and Sunday night. We're on every church committee." He didn't say, "Ye must observe religious duties." He said, "Ye must be born again."

You see, some people's idea of the new birth is adhering to what their father did and what their grandfather did. But God has no grandchildren. Each one of us must be born again for ourselves.

Many people have only an intellectual conception of the Lord Jesus Christ. "I believe in Jesus," they will say. But is He your Lord and Savior? "Well, I believe in Him." Have you been born again? "Well, I believe Jesus, you know. I believe in God." The devil believes in Jesus. The devil believes in God.

Even some of the worst sinners believe in God and the Bible. When they get into a crisis situation, you'd be amazed at what comes out of their mouth — the Bible. They'll quote anything they can think of. They get in a motor car with a friend and he's doing 120 miles an hour, they start quoting scripture. "The Lord is my Shepherd, I shall not want." But that won't save them. Jesus said, "Ye must be born again."

"Well, Brother Rodney, I'm a moral person," some will say. "If God is God how can all the good people in the world, go to hell?" Because Jesus said, "Ye must be born again."

"But look at Brother Joe Blow. He was a good man. He didn't rob from anybody. He wouldn't even hurt a flea. Do you know that if he found a bug in the house, he'd go and pick it up and nicely put it out. What a moral man. What a man of high standing in the community. Fifty years of marriage to the same woman. His children — one is a doctor, the other one's a lawyer.

They were all well respected. Do you mean to say he's going to hell?" Jesus said, "Ye must be born again."

You can't be born again until you realize your need to be born again. And you can't realize your need to be born again until you come face to face with the Lord Jesus. The Bible says there is a way that seems right to man but the end thereof is death (Proverbs 14:12). We have plenty of cultured, refined, moral people, but unless they are born again, they're going to split hell wide open.

There Is a Heaven to Gain and a Hell to Shun

> **There was a certain rich man, which was clothed in purple and fine linen, and fared sumptuously every day:**
>
> **And there was a certain beggar named Lazarus, which was laid at his gate, full of sores,**
>
> **And desiring to be fed with the crumbs which fell from the rich man's table: moreover the dogs came and licked his sores.**
>
> **And it came to pass, that the beggar died, and was carried by the angels into Abraham's bosom: the rich man also died, and was buried;**
>
> **And in hell he lift up his eyes, being in torments, and seeth Abraham afar off, and Lazarus in his bosom.**

And he cried and said, Father Abraham, have mercy on me, and send Lazarus, that he may dip the tip of his finger in water, and cool my tongue; for I am tormented in this flame.

But Abraham said, Son, remember that thou in thy lifetime receivedst thy good things, and likewise Lazarus evil things: but now he is comforted and thou art tormented.

And beside all this, between us and you there is a great gulf fixed: so that they which would pass from hence to you cannot; neither can they pass to us, that would come from thence.

Then he said, I pray thee therefore, father, that thou wouldst send him to my father's house:

For I have five brethren; that he may testify unto them, lest they also come into this place of torment.

Abraham saith unto him, They have Moses and the prophets; let them hear them.

And he said, Nay, father Abraham: but if one went unto them from the dead, they will repent.

And he said unto him, If they hear not Moses and the prophets, neither will they be persuaded, though one rose from the dead.

Luke 16:19-31

This was not a parable. Jesus said, "There was a rich man." This actually happened. The rich man, who had never begged in his whole life, died and he went down to hell. Lazarus was the beggar who had nothing. All he could do was eat the scraps from the rich man's table. He died and was carried into Abraham's bosom.

The rich man was in torment. This tells me that hell is a place of torment and that heaven is a place of rest and peace. The earth is the only hell that the child of God will ever know; the earth is the only heaven the sinner will ever know.

The Bible says it's appointed unto man (...once to die, but after that the judgment (Hebrews 9:27). There are people who are committing suicide and they're thinking that they're going to end their life and go into blessing and peace. They go from the frying pan into the fire. They go straight into hell, a place of eternal damnation and eternal torment.

Did you know they're trying to pass laws in the state of California where it's illegal for a preacher to preach on hell because he's causing duress on people's emotional state? They're trying to pass laws in this country where it's illegal to preach the gospel and bring people to a place of decision.

If they ever pass that law, they're going to have to lock the door and throw away the key on me, because I am not going to quit preaching the truth of the Gospel of the Lord Jesus Christ. I'm going to tell people there's a heaven to gain and a hell to shun. Hell wasn't made for man. Hell wasn't made for God's people. Hell was made for the devil and his angels.

Those who are in hell right now — given the opportunity — would want to come out because of the torment. But if you told them, "When you come out, you must accept Jesus," they would turn Jesus down. That's why they must go to a lost eternity. It's not because God wants to keep them there, but because they do not want to accept Jesus Christ as their Lord and Savior.

The rich man said, "If you would send someone out to talk to my five brothers, they would believe." Abraham said, "They have Moses and the prophets. They didn't believe them, why are they going to believe someone back from the dead?"

The rich man never begged in this life. Lazarus begged in this life. But the rich man became a beggar in the life to come. I'd rather be a beggar in this life and not beg in the life to come, than be someone who does not beg in this life but must beg in eternal life. He was begging for a drop of water to cool his tongue. He was begging that Abraham would send somebody to go and speak to his brothers. But even someone from the dead would not convince some people of their need to be born again.

My schoolmates used to mock me and say, "You've wasted your whole life serving God. You don't run to the parties, you don't get drunk like us."

I said, "First of all, I don't want to do that because I love Jesus and I'm having great fun anyway. But let's say, just for argument's sake, that there is no God. Let's say there is no eternity. When I die and you die, we've lost nothing.

"But what if there is a God and there is a heaven and a hell? When I die, I'm going straight to be with the Lord. What will you do when you stand before the Almighty God? What will you say then? God will take you back to this day when you and I were talking face to face and you told me it's a bunch of hogwash. You'll spend the rest of eternity in hell realizing the opportunities you've missed."

Hell is a place of torment. The people there are going see the missed opportunities they had to accept Jesus.

I shudder to think of people who have come to our meetings and stormed out because they didn't want to accept Jesus as Savior. In hell they will remember and say, "O God, if only, if only, if only." The reason they have to go there is not because God wants to punish people but because they do not want to accept Jesus Christ as their Lord and Savior.

There's only one way to God. The new birth is through one door and that's Jesus Christ. The new birth is not through Mohammed. The new birth is not through Buddha. The new birth is not through Confucius.

The difference between Jesus Christ and Buddha and Mohammed and Confucius is you can go to Buddha's grave today and it's full. You can go to Mohammed's grave today and it's full. You can go to Confucius' grave today — it's also full.

But the grave of the Lord Jesus Christ is empty! He is risen. The stone is rolled away. That's what makes Christianity different from every other cult and every other religion. Jesus Christ is alive. He is risen! If He hadn't risen, Christianity would be like every other cult. But He rose from the dead.

Jesus rose and He's coming back again. When He left the earth, the angels said the same Jesus you're seeing go now is coming back (Acts 1:11).

If You Were Arrested for Being a Christian

The Bible says, "If any man be in Christ, he is a new creature: old things are passed away" (Second Corinthians 5:17). But if you look at some Christians, there's no telling that they've passed from death unto life.

I heard one preacher ask, "If you were arrested for being a Christian, would there be enough evidence against your life to convict you?" Some Christians would get off on probation. Others would get life sentences without the chance of parole.

Chapter 3

The New Birth Brings Change

There was a man of the Pharisees, named Nicodemus, a ruler of the Jews:

The same came to Jesus by night, and said unto him, Rabbi, we know that thou art a teacher come from God: for no man can do these miracles that thou doest, except God be with him.

Jesus answered and said unto him, Verily, verily, I say unto thee, Except a man be born again, he cannot see the kingdom of God.

Nicodemus saith unto him, How can a man be born when he is old? can he enter a second time into his mother's womb and be born?

John 3:1-4

People who try to understand the new birth intellectually, are reasoning with their minds. Like Nicodemus, they are trying to understand how we can be born a second time. Some would say this born-again experience is something new. No, it's not. Jesus spoke about it long ago.

Jesus answered, Verily, verily, I say unto thee, Except a man be born of water and of

the Spirit, he cannot enter into the kingdom of God.

That which is born of the flesh is flesh; and that which is born of the Spirit is spirit.

Marvel not that I said unto thee, Ye must be born again.

The wind bloweth where it listeth, and thou hearest the sound thereof, but canst tell whence it cometh, and whither it goeth: so is every one that is born of the Spirit.

Nicodemus answered and said unto him, How can these things be?

Jesus answered and said unto him, Art thou a master of Israel, and knowest not these things?

Verily, verily, I say unto thee, We speak that we do know, and testify that we have seen; and ye receive not our witness.

If I have told you earthly things, and ye believe not, how shall ye believe, if I tell you of heavenly things?

And no man hath ascended up to heaven, but he that came down from heaven, even the Son of man which is in heaven.

And as Moses lifted up the serpent in the wilderness, even so must the Son of man be lifted up:

That whosoever believeth in him should not perish, but have eternal life.

For God so loved the world, that he gave his only begotten Son, that whosoever believeth in him should not perish, but have everlasting life.

For God sent not his Son into the world to condemn the world; but that the world through him might be saved.

He that believeth on him is not condemned: but he that believeth not is condemned already, because he hath not believed in the name of the only begotten Son of God.

And this is the condemnation, that light is come into the world, and men loved darkness rather than light, because their deeds were evil.

For every one that doeth evil hateth the light, neither cometh to the light, lest his deeds should be reproved.

But he that doeth truth cometh to the light, that his deeds may be made manifest, that they are wrought in God.

John 3:5-21

When you accept Jesus Christ as your Lord and Savior, something takes place. There's a literal change made in you. That's why I have difficulty believing that some people are truly born again. I don't see a change. First Peter 1:23 says, "Being born again, not of corruptible seed, but of incorruptible, by the word of God, which liveth and abideth for ever."

When you come into contact with God, something is going to happen in your life. There's going to be a radical change. Everyone will be able to look at you and see the change, not because you wear a T-shirt saying, "Honk if you love Jesus." Not because you have a fish on your forehead or you carry a big Bible. But they should see, just by your presence, that something about you is different. In other words, when you meet up with God, you change. The new birth means change.

When you have an encounter with God your life is going to change. Don't tell me you've had an encounter with God if you're suing your Christian brother. I won't believe you. The Bible says that we know that we have passed from death unto life because we love the brethren (First John 3:14).

If someone is born again, you're going to see it. You're going to hear it. Everything about that person will be different. When they're involved in sin, they'll dress like the world, they'll talk like the world, they'll hang out with the world, they'll mix with sinners and feel comfortable there and the sinners will feel comfortable with them too.

But when Jesus comes inside, He cleans the house out. Your lifestyle will be affected. You start loving people. Your marriage gets turned around. Your finances get healed. Your sick bodies get healed. That's what the new birth does.

Was it just a mental prayer that you prayed and said, "Jesus come into my life and forgive me of my sins"? You did it because you didn't want to go to hell. Or do you know the time and the place when you had an encounter with God and your life changed radically? Can you say, "I was going in the wrong direction. I was heading for a lost eternity and the Lord Jesus Christ came to me and I accepted Him. I turned my back on sin in the world. I repented and I chose to go the other way."

If I stood on the interstate in the middle of the road and a Mack truck came down the road at 65 miles an hour and hit me head on, my friends and family would peel me off the front grill of that truck. The first thing they're going to say to me is "Rodney, you've changed. You look different, Rodney. You talk different. You walk different. You're not the same person we've known. What happened to you?"

I had an encounter. I'm changed. I'm different. Have you had a "Mack truck" experience that revolutionized your life? Do you know the day and the hour that you crossed over from death unto life?

The Bible says we've been delivered out of the kingdom of darkness and translated into the kingdom of His dear Son (Colossians 1:13).

There's an actual transition. Something takes place. And everyone can see it. There's something different about you.

But we have people in the church who say, "I'm a born-again bank robber, Brother Rodney. I rob banks part time. Brother, I'm a born-again Mafia hit man. I'm born again and I deal in cocaine on the side. I really feel I need to support the church. I'm born again, Brother Rodney, and I race horses on the side."

I used to think every Christian had angels' wings and halos. One day I looked and saw the halo wasn't there. It was two little horns coming out of their head. Some Christians have the symbol of the fish, but they should put a shark on their car, not a fish. Just when you thought it was safe to go back to church!

Christians are ripping each other off. Sometimes I'd rather go to a sinner in business because at least I know I can shout at him if he does a bad job. If you go to the Christian and he does a bad job, (you) are expected (to) pay the money and walk in love. At least with the sinner you can say, "You Philistine, thou hast not done the job correctly."

When sinners can come to church and feel like it's a great place and sit there week after week and never give their lives to Jesus, you know that church is a compromise. When sinners walk in the door, they should be affected immediately. They should sense the presence of God and they should be convicted — not condemned — and should want to repent.

It's the Goodness of God that Leads to Repentance

The Bible says it's the goodness of God that leads us to repentance (Romans 2:4). I think repentance has become a bad word today. If you talk about repenting in the church you'd think you'd just cussed. Some people will bawl crocodile tears and say, "Oh, I'm so sorry. I'll never do it again, Brother Rodney, I'll never do it again." You pray with them and they go right out the door and do it again. They didn't repent!

Jesus said, "All that the Father giveth me shall come to me; and him that cometh to me I will in no wise cast out" (John 6:37). God doesn't reject you, He accepts you. Yet there are ministers who think they're John the Baptist and they want to knock people over the head all the time and hope that they're going to come in and get saved.

Even an old hog has enough brains to know that if every time he goes to drink from a water trough, a brick falls on his head — he shouldn't drink there anymore. And people wonder why no one wants to come to church. It's because the preacher beats them up.

The Bible says it's the goodness of God that leads to repentance. The Bible also says,

Lord shall be saved" (Romans 10:13). God will not cast anyone away.

You may say, "Brother Rodney, I've had it with that person. I'm at the end of my rope with that person." The end of your rope is the beginning of God's rope. Where your grace ends, God's grace begins. Where your mercy ends, God's mercy begins. Where your love ends, the love of God begins.

Some Christians are a terrible advertisement for the Lord Jesus Christ. In actual fact, I wouldn't send some Christians to help someone on the brink of suicide. The man's standing at the top of a 30-story building about to jump off. You send some believer there and the man will take one look at them and say, "That's it. I thought there might be hope, but now that I look at his face I know there's no hope."

Too many Christians are walking around looking like a bomb hit them. "I'm saved, Brother Rodney." Saved from what? "I've been in the Way for forty years." It's time you got out of the way so we can move on.

Some people believe First John 1:9 is for the sinner. "If we confess our sins, he is faithful and just to forgive us our sins." That's not written to the sinner; it's written to the Church. If a 40-year-old sinner had to confess his sins, he'd have a lot of sins to confess. It would take him another 40 years to confess his sins. It's for the believer to confess his sins.

God doesn't find out about your sins when you confess them. Some people think when they go to God and say, "Lord, I've sinned," God says, "My, I didn't know that." God is not surprised by your sin. He's waiting for you to confess them so He can forgive them.

Sin separates. You watch people who were on fire for God and suddenly they get into an area of deception and they open themselves up to sin. The devil knocks them in the head and they go into an area of sin and then they stop going to church.

Romans 10:8, 9 says, "But what saith it? the word is nigh thee, even in thy mouth, and in thy heart: that is, the word of faith, which we preach; That if thou shalt confess with thy mouth the Lord Jesus, and shalt believe in thine heart that God hath raised him from the dead, thou shalt be saved."

God wants you to run to Him, not from Him. If you confess with your mouth the Lord Jesus, believe in your heart that God raised him from the dead, you will be saved. That is what gets us born again.

> **For with the heart man believeth unto righteousness: and with the mouth confession is made unto salvation.**

For the scripture sayeth, Whosoever believeth in him shall not be ashamed.

For there is no difference between the Jew and the Greek: for the same Lord over all is rich unto all that call upon him.

For whosoever shall call upon the name of the Lord shall be saved.

How then shall they call on him in whom they have not believed? and how shall they believe in him of whom they have not heard? and how shall they hear without a preacher?

And how shall they preach, except they be sent? as it is written, How beautiful are the feet of them that preach the gospel of peace, and bring glad tidings of good things!

Romans 10:10-15

But as many as received him, to them gave he power to become the sons of God.

John 1:12

God has a plan for your life. Accept Jesus today, come as you are, and allow Jesus to come into your heart.

Pray this prayer right now:

Father, I come to You in the precious name of Jesus. Lord, You said in Your Word that if I confess with my mouth Jesus is Lord and I believe with my heart that God raised Him from the dead, I will be saved. So Father, I confess right now Jesus Christ is my Lord and my Savior.

Lord Jesus, come into my heart. I repent of all my sins. Wash me in Your precious blood and cleanse me of all my sin. I turn my back on the world. I will serve You from this day onwards. Thank You for changing my life. Amen.

Sermon Outline:

What It Means to be Born Again

Foundation Scripture: John 3:16

1. *Needs to be a greater understanding of the New Birth.*
    a. 2 Corinthians 5:17
    b. A New Creation
    c. Colossians 1:13
2. *My Name is Written Down.*
    a. Luke 10:17-20
    b. Proverbs 14:12
    c. Luke 16:19-31
3. *The New Birth Brings Change.*
    a. John 3:1-4
    b. John 3:5-21
    c. 1 Peter 1:23
    d. 1 John 3:14
    e. Romans 10:8-10